The Boy Who Saved the Whale

Written and Illustrated by Kelly Mrocki

www.alysbooks.com

The Boy Who Saved the Whale

Copyright © Kelly Mrocki
Illustration copyright © Kelly Mrocki

First Edition 2017
Published by Aly's Books

www.alysbooks.com
Your Book | Our Mission

Designed by Fish Biscuit

All rights reserved. No part of this book may be reproduced or transmitted in any form or by any means, electronic, mechanical, photocopying or otherwise without the prior permission of the publisher.

ISBN: 978-0-6480017-4-4

For my son Josh who is helping to protect our wonderful marine life. I am so proud of you

I found a little whale
and kept it as a pet.

I placed it in my bathtub,
and tried to keep it wet.

I taught it lots of tricks, and
I told it what to do,
If you had a pet whale,
wouldn't you do that too?

I gave it lots of food,
sandwiches and ice cream.

I named my whale George – he's a sight to be seen.

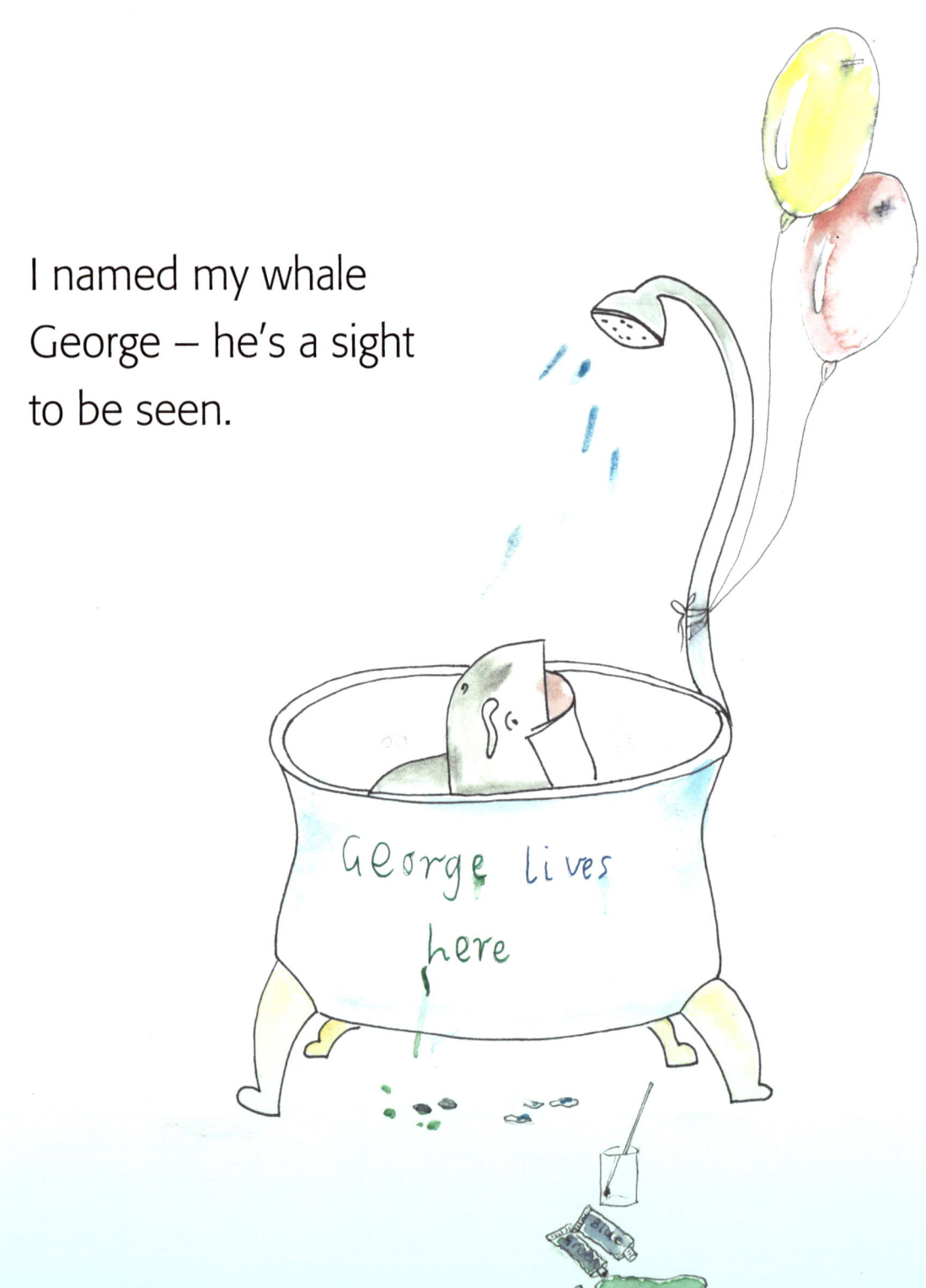

George swam around in circles, he splashed and thrashed about.
It must be 'cause he's happy here, of that I have no doubt.

I invited all my friends to take photos and have a ride,
I even charged them an entry fee to sit with him and smile.

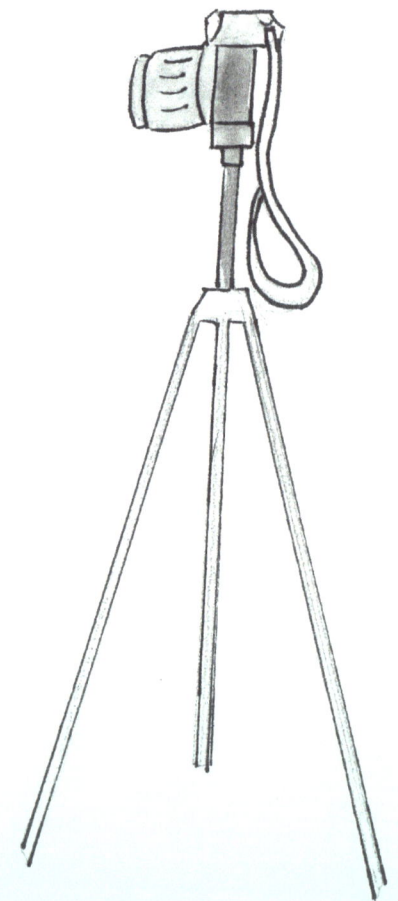

I made a lot of money, and I bought a lot of toys,
Some of them I gave to George, but he didn't get much joy.

When I looked back at the photos, George seemed kind of sad.
His fin was bent and droopy, his skin was patchy and drab.

That night I had a dream, with songs of the deep dark sea. A whale was dancing on the waves, jumping high with glee.

I woke up in the morning, and I knew just what to do.
Why did it take me so long to figure out the clues?

It made me all excited, my tummy filled with knots,
It's something that I have to do, but I'm going to miss him lots.

I ran to visit George – he'd had the same dream too. "Don't worry, I'm taking you home," I said, "back to the deep blue."

I rushed George to the ocean, to his beautiful home in the sea.

I watched the waves carry him.
"Don't worry now, you're free."

George splashed around and grinned, he jumped up in the air.

He sang a song so loudly
that it prickled up my hair.

AWOOOo o
AWoooo°

"Thank you," moaned the whale as the little boy walked away,
"For knowing that all I need in life is right here in this bay."

Josh turned around and smiled – "You're welcome," he replied. "Knowing you has been a thrill, and one magical ride!"

The little boy had saved the whale, it was the right thing to do. Because if you had a pet whale, wouldn't you do that too?!

Whales, dolphins, and all kinds of sea animals are caught and kept captive in marine parks all over the world. They are often subjected to cruelty, food deprivation and isolation.

Sea Shepherd Conservation Society is a non-profit organisation with a mission to end habitat destruction and the slaughter of wildlife in the world's oceans.

You can show your support by visiting the Sea Shepherd fleets in Williamstown while at port. They run ship tours on weekends and are a great resource to teach people about protecting our sea life. All crewmembers are volunteers, and they appreciate food donations for their missions at sea. Sea Shepherd has fleets all over the world protecting our endangered marine life.

Please check their websites for more information.

www.seashepherd.org.au
www.seashepherdglobal.org

Sign a petition! There are many petitions on the web for marine conservation.

Check out **www.marineconservation.org.au**
Some to look out for are:

illegal whaling, Taiji dolphin hunts, super trawlers, oil drilling, export of shark fins, plastic bag ban, cash for containers. This is just to name a few.

At 6 years of age, Josh sent a petition to the Australian government with over 300 signatures, pleading for them to take action against whaling boats in and around Australian waters. He has sent letters to the Japanese government begging them to end their whaling programs. Josh has donated his birthday money to purchase food for Sea Shepherd volunteers, and whenever he can, Josh will pick up rubbish and left over fishing wire on our beaches so that it doesn't end up back in the ocean.

Remember to keep our beaches clean, use less plastic, and recycle, recycle, recycle!

Teachers Notes

Activities to be linked to this story.

- Take some time outside to watch wildlife. Look under rocks to observe centipedes, slaters, snails and other creatures. Sit very still and see what birds or butterflies land nearby. Listen to the sounds of nature.

- Plant native trees and shrubs in the playground to support local wildlife.

- Have books available for children to observe animals in their natural habitats

- Create a native table with different habitats such as: water, gum tree branches, rocks and sand. Include native animals such as: koalas, fish, lizards, crabs and birds. Let the children match the animal to their habitat.

- Take photos of animals that live around your centre. See if the children can identify them in books or online.

Teaching compassion for animals can help children develop empathy for all living things.

Respecting animal habitats is an important part of teaching children about caring for the environment.

This book ties in nicely with the National Quality Framework for Early Childhood Education and Care.

Early Years Learning Framework

Outcome 2.

Children are connected with and contribute to their world.

- Children become socially responsible and show respect for the environment.

National Quality Standard

QA 3.3 The service takes an active role in caring for its environment and contributes to a sustainable future.

3.3.2 Children are supported to become environmentally responsible and show respect for the environment.

A Healthier Home

These products are a great way to keep your home clean and toxic free

Bi-Carb Soda (Baking Soda) is an excellent deodorizer, but it can also be used to scrub sinks and clean toilets.

Vinegar (White distilled) is great for deodorizing, degreasing and general cleaning.

You can use it diluted with water or you can add drops of lavender or Eucalyptus oil.

Vinegar is extremely inexpensive and readily available.

Essential Oils can contain anti-bacterial properties and can be added to your cleaners for extra strength.

Air Freshener

Ingredients

Lavender Essential Oils
Water

Method

Step 1. Fill a squirt bottle with water
Step 2. Add 5-10 drops of Lavender Essential Oils and shake to combine

Home Made liquid laundry detergent

Ingredients and equipment:

Bucket
7.5 litres of water
½ cup washing soda (Soda Ash)
½ cup baking soda
¾ cup liquid castile soap
20 drops of your favourite essential oils
Large spoon to stir
Glass containers to store finished liquid

Method

Step 1. Add half a cup of washing soda to the bucket and add just enough hot water to cover the washing soda. Stir well to dissolve.
Step 2. Pour half a cup of baking soda into the water/washing soda mixture and stir well to dissolve.
Step 3. Fill up your bucket with hot tap water, but leave about half an inch of room on top.
Step 4. Add ¾ cup of castile soap
Step 5. Pour in approx 20 drops of your favourite essential oils.
Step 6. Carefully stir everything together until well mixed.
Step 7. Pour the detergent into glass containers.

To use: Give the container a shake before use as some settling can occur; this will dissolve in the wash so don't be too concerned. Pour 1/3 cup of the detergent in with your dirty clothes and wash as normal. **Keep out of reach of children.** Although this is an all-natural product, it is highly alkaline (to remove the grime).

(Disclaimer: While this page is intended as a general information resource and all care has been taken in compiling the contents, it does not take account of individual circumstances and is not intended as a substitute for professional advice. The author and the publisher cannot be held responsible for any claim or action that may arise from reliance on the information contained on this page. Please follow instructions and measurements carefully as use of different quantities may have unintended consequences. Test patch all surfaces before wide spread use).

A special thank you to the following people for supporting this book

Charlie Mrocki; Ashley Mrocki; Bobbie Williamson; Terry and Sue Williamson; Denise and Rex Chadwick; Lauren Gillett; Shane, Shannon, Aiden and Chloe Williamson; Elliot and Willow Bodor; Aunty Neila Williamson; Harry Williamson; Mama and Papa Dunn; Daniel and Emma Williamson; Sharon, Mark, Joel and Ryan Kuperholz; Martin Mulvany; Alana and Caitlyn Crawford; Zoe and Charlie Robin; Olivia-Rose Bills; Adele and Isla Denton; Mila and Will McHugh; Sue and Julian Downes; The Eardley Family; Kerry Verdon; Rosie and Theo Egan; The Bushettes Number 1 Coach; Estelle, Iris and Edward; The De Valle family; The Watters Family; Sonny and Maeve Chadwick; Leanne; Jeffrey Loy; Clare, Jade and Lisa Airs; Maggie and June Warren; Deborah Bail, April Rainey and William Rainey; Alexander Athanasakos; Kathy Morriss and Family; Lionel Mrocki and Karen Amos; Tilly and Kitty Parish; Olivia and Poppy Skerry; Emily and Daniel Lukins; Liliana, Daniel, Nikola and Marija Janev; Gemma, Sam and Lucy Porter; John and Margaret Gordon; Pop and Bern; Steph Swan; Dominic Greene; The Yze Family; Maree and Harry; Claudia, Hamish and Isla Baxter; Christos, Arthur and Kimon Costopoulos; Phoebe Apted; Anaya and Aryan Reddy; William and Jakob Inness; Sea Shepherd; Xander, Mac and Amelie Chisholm; Charlie and Ashton Mellett; Revaant and Tenay Toshniwal

A special thank you to Estelle and Olivia-Rose for the beautiful whale drawings used in the Teachers Notes section

Notes

You might like to help protect an animal from this list, just like Josh did.

Endangered animals in Australia
Tasmanian Devil
Mountain Pygmy Possum
Leadbeater's Possum
Eastern Barred Bandicoot
Orange Bellied Parrot
Southern Bent Wing Bat
New Holland Mouse
Smoky Mouse
Brush Tailed Rock Wallaby
Northern Hairy Nosed Wombat
Helmeted Honeyeater
Gilbert's Potoroo
Regent Honeyeater
Grassland Earless Dragon
Guthega Skink
Alpine She Oak Skink
Hawksbill Turtle
Corroboree Frog (and about 14 other species of frog)
Many fish, insects, crustaceans, molluscs and corals

Endangered animals around the world
Rhinoceros
Tigers
Orang-utans
Gorillas
Whales
Elephants
Chimpanzees
Galapagos Penguins
Giant Pandas
Many species of turtles
Sea Lions
Snow Leopard
And sadly, many more…

Notes

Notes

www.ingramcontent.com/pod-product-compliance
Lightning Source LLC
Chambersburg PA
CBHW042144290426
44110CB00002B/106